CREATED 4 WORSHIP

Charleston, SC
www.PalmettoPublishing.com

Created 4 Worship

First Edition

Hardcover ISBN: 978-1-64990-886-5
Paperback ISBN: 978-1-64990-757-8
eBook ISBN: 978-1-64990-544-4

Created 4 Worship

DR. MARK ROWDEN, TH.D

Contents

This book is dedicated to and in memory of my natural father, the late Troy Lee Rowden. He taught me the importance of discipline, not knowing that teaching me discipline in the natural helped nurture me to embrace spiritual discipline from my heavenly Father. To be a true worshipper, one must be spiritually disciplined.

Introduction

It was the summer of 1967, and I was a small lad, sitting on the pew between my mother, Lela Mae Rowden, and my aunt Lena Faye Darby during a worship service at the Fourth Missionary Baptist Church in Houston Texas, where the pastor, Rev. E. Stanley Branch, was preaching the service. At the tender age of six, I didn't understand seeing members lifting their hands while the preacher spoke. As a child, it seemed out of order to me hearing people shout out "Amen" periodically, while the preacher spoke. I was taught as a child to sit still, keep quiet, and behave myself while in church. On this particular Sunday, I cannot remember what the preacher preached about, but there was a different atmosphere this particular day. I felt different than on previous Sundays. I recall after the worship service while the congregants were all leaving, some gathered near the altar to greet the pastor. There I stood, a small, little six-year-old boy pulling on the pastor's robe. As he looked down at me, with tears in my eyes, I said to him, "I want to be baptized."

He looked at me and asked, "Where are your parents?"

I replied, "I don't know, but I want to get baptized." He commanded that I go get my parents and bring them to him. My father never attended church service with us for as long as I can remember; it was my mother and her sister who took us to church Sunday after Sunday. I went to get my mom who was already standing on the outside looking as if she were looking for someone. I beckoned her and said, "Mama, come go with me." She inquired as to where I had been. I again asked her to come go with me to see the pastor. It was that day she agreed to have the pastor baptize me. Not realizing it then, but it was the beginning of a worship journey God would take me on, one that I shall never forget.

The Greek word for worship is *proskynéō* (from 4314 */prós*, "towards," and *kyneo*, "*to kiss*") —properly, to kiss the ground when prostrating before a superior; to ***worship***, ready "to fall down/prostrate oneself to adore on one's knees" (*DNTT*); to "do obeisance" (*BAGD*). 4352 (*proskyneō*) has been (metaphorically) described as "the kissing-ground" between believers (the Bride) and Christ (the heavenly Bridegroom). While this is true, 4352 (*proskynéō*) suggests the willingness to make all necessary physical *gestures of obeisance.*] (Strong's Hebrew Greek Dictionary). From the above definition, I have always thought that I had to bow down or lay prostrate at the altar in order for it to be worship. Little did I know there are many ways to prostrate for *worshipping* God as long as it is *in spirit and in truth.*

Years had passed, and the family's participation in church services slowly declined. In fact, the only time I recall attending church was during the summer while visiting with my grandmother, Mrs. Perdis Jones, a woman of incredible faith. She sang in the choir in a little country church in the small town of Willisville, Arkansas (my father's hometown). Boy, were the church services different from what I was used to in the city of Houston! These people were singing and praising and clapping their hands. The sound of tambourines rang out like nothing I'd heard. But that is not what captured my attention the most; it was when a woman began shouting and jumping, and her hair fell off her head. Yes, I realized it was a wig, but as a young teen I laughed because I thought it to be so funny. This was yet another turning point for me on my worship journey.

Years later, as I went off into the military, once again my participation in church declined. However, I became a member of a fraternal organization while serving overseas in Germany, and its members attended worship services often. So there I was, now a young adult, barely out of my teens back in the presence of God. Seems there was no escaping His presence. But I was still missing something in my spiritual walk. The journey I knew God had me on promised so much more. Several years had passed, and after returning from a combat tour in Operation Desert Shield/Storm, I was deployed to yet another overseas tour, this time in Southwest Asia, Seoul, South Korea. It was during the fall of 1993, and a military promotion lead to my being sent to Fort Gordon, Georgia to attend a military school. Five years previously my mother was called home from labor to reward, having lived fifty-five years before a long illness claimed her life. Since I was in the United States, I made it my business to go home and visit my father. While there, I decided to treat myself by going out to the bar for a drink. Though baptized and attending church, I still had a ways to go in my spiritual walk. My recollection of how that night began is so very clear to this day. I was sitting at the bar, sipping on a strawberry wine cooler. The music was blaring; the half-naked dancers were dancing; people all around me were talking, and it seemed like I could hear all of their conversations at the same time. It was as if the entire room slowed down. I could see myself sitting at the bar as if I were out of my body, watching me. I remember dropping my head, and I began to pray. I said, "Lord, I am tired of living like this. Please remove this life from me." Immediately, I felt the Holy Spirit come over me. I slowly pushed that good tasting strawberry wine cooler away from me. I got up and walked out of the bar and went to my father's house.

It was there in the family room as I lay on the sofa that my mother had once laid on for years that I fell into a deep sleep. While I slept, it became a Pauline moment when he said, "I knew a man in Christ above fourteen years ago, (whether in the body, I cannot tell, or whether out of the body, I cannot tell: God knoweth) such as one caught up to the third heaven." 2 Corinthians 12:1 (KJV).

As I lay there, a man appeared to me. I could not see him, only a shadow walking beside me with his arm around my shoulder. We were walking down a dirt road, and in the distance I saw three men working on a building doing construction that looked like a church. The shadow walking beside me opened his voice and spoke as clearly as someone talking to me in the natural and said, "They are building this church for you—GO!!! And preach my gospel, and low, I am with you always."

I immediately woke from this deep sleep, a sleep like I'd never experienced, with my hands stretched towards heaven shouting, "I will serve the Lord; I will serve the Lord!!!!" Unsure of what I had just experienced, I said audibly, "Lord, if this is you speaking to me, show me in your Word." The family always kept a large family Bible on the coffee table in front of the sofa I was on. And as I lifted that Bible and without turning pages, I opened it to Matthew 28:18-19, "*Go ye therefore, and teach all nations, baptizing them in the name of the Father, and of the Son, and of the Holy Ghost: Teaching them to observe all things whatsoever I have commanded you: and, lo, I am with you always, [even] unto the end of the world." Amen.*

The spirit of God was so overwhelming that I felt a need to be baptized again. My home pastor was away at a convention so I shared my experience with one of the associate ministers and told him I wanted to get baptized again. I was expecting the encouragement I was seeking; instead I was crushed to hear him say, "You don't need to get baptized again 'one Lord, one faith, and one baptism.'"

I called my Aunt Gladys in Arkansas and explained my spiritual experience and what the minister had told me. She encouraged me by saying, "Son, he's trying to do God's business. You find someone who will baptize you and get baptized if you feel a need to do so." I called Pastor Leon Smith in Atlanta, Georgia (who later became my father in the ministry) and shared my spiritual experience with him. He told me if I could come to Atlanta, he would baptize me.

I jumped in my car and drove twelve hours to Atlanta, Georgia. When I got there, Pastor Smith said I needed to go on a fast. I had never fasted before in my life; I had never been exposed to what a spiritual fast was all about. He explained to me what fasting meant and its spiritual importance. I agreed because I knew something was different in my life, though not knowing the challenge I was about to face. In the days leading up to the baptism, there was a worship service in Griffin, Georgia. Elder Smith instructed me to attend the worship service. His sister-in-law, Elder Fleta Daniel, was kind enough to drive me to the worship service. While driving on the highway to Griffin, the traffic was extremely backed up. Fleta said she was going to exit the highway and take a back road; she said she wasn't sure where the road would lead, but she knew it would get us to Griffin. As we traveled down this narrow country road, a road where cows were crossing the street, I thought it strange to see cows unattended, crossing the road. We had to slow down to allow them to cross. As I looked ahead, I could see in the short distance what looked like a house being built; the closer we got, it became clearer that it was a church being built, and there were three men building it. Immediately, I began to weep bitterly. It was the exact same vision I had seen in my dream when the Holy Spirit spoke to me back in Houston.

It was yet another confirmation as to what God had in store for me. When we arrived at the worship service, I stood in the back still trying to wrap my mind around what was happening to me spiritually. While the guest evangelist was preaching, he began to prophesy during a spiritual impartation moment. He said, "Young man, come forth." He was looking and pointing towards me. Being raised in a traditional Baptist church, I was all the way in the back of the church because I was not used to this type of worship service: even the shouting and wigs flying off in my grandmother's country church did not compare. He yelled it again, "Young man, come forth."

I looked behind me and the only thing behind me was the wall. I said to myself… 'of all of the people in this place, why in heaven is this man calling me? He doesn't even know me.' I pointed to myself as if saying, "are you talking to me?" He nodded his head in the affirmative. I walked slowly through the crowd of worshippers, hoping he would lose sight of me in this extremely spiritual moment flowing through the service. All of a sudden it was as if the crowd disappeared; the room slowed down, and it was only he and I standing there. As I stood in front of the evangelist, he instructed me to lift up both my hands. In obedience, I did. He then spoke to me saying, "God has called you to preach his Word, and I am going to anoint your hands because of how you will use them to lay hands in ministry." As he anointed my hands, one at a time, back and forth, I begin to shout. It was the first time I'd ever shouted in jubilation in a worship service and the second time shouting from the depths of my soul.

Tears began to run down my face because I was certain of what God was doing in me, and I was still afraid to step out into total faith in the experience. If that wasn't enough to cause me to want to walk away and say I am not ready for this, the day of the baptism finally arrived. It seemed like I had been waiting a month of Sundays when it actually had only been a few days. I was excited that the reason I went to Atlanta in the first place was finally here. As I walked into the baptismal pool and looked out at the small crowd, I could see Pastor Gloria Smith (wife of Pastor Leon Smith) and mother Lannie Brownlee looking at me with anticipation in their eyes. I knew this was it. As Pastor Smith took me down into the water and brought me back up, I felt like what I read in the Bible when John the Baptist baptized Jesus. It was as if a dove had landed on me. I felt a spiritual cleansing like never before and then came from my mouth the third shout of jubilation from such a spiritual experience.

But as I stood there, water running down my face mixed with tears of joy, there was an older pastor standing there named Bishop Hoke; he shouted at me, "Young man, your troubles have just begun!"

All I could think of was, "You're kidding me." After all of this, you mean to tell me trouble lies ahead? I didn't understand it then, but over the course of the years, it has become quite clear. It was that very moment that led me to share how important it is, as well as the difficulties for some to understand, that we were "Created to Worship."

John 4:23, 24 NLT

The writer, John, identifies a couple of crucial points about Jesus. First, Jesus made it a point to clarify the meaning of worship. The Samaritan woman endeavored to distract Jesus from her sin by asking Him to resolve an old spiritual argument. It was a question of where proper worship should take place: Mount Gerizim or the temple in Jerusalem. Rather than taking the bait, Jesus declares that "true" worship of God is not tied to a specific location, but it is tied to one's heart. This speaks volumes about the Samaritan woman. Her lifestyle was deeply immoral (John 4:16–18), so much so that she seems to have been cast out, even among the outcast Samaritans. Jesus's encounter with Nicodemus, the educated and powerful Pharisee, gave cause for humility in order to be opened to God. (John 3:9–12) This woman, like so many of us, needed to know that she was wanted, loved, and valued. Jesus will always meet us where we are.

The Samaritan woman came to the well looking to quench her spiritual thirst with a series of failed relationships. At first, she did not understand what Jesus meant by a spring of living water, never to thirst again. (John 4:13–14) Based on what she says in the next verse, it seems to be dawning on her what Jesus is really speaking of. The conversation in this scripture is very rewarding for those experiencing a thirst after Jesus, a hunger for true worship in their lives. 2 Chronicles, chapters six and seven, are a reminder of how we should approach God in worship through sacrifice. The people sacrificed 122,000 cattle and sheep. This was their way of approaching God. God has to accept our worship; God has to approve our worship. As you read through the chapters of this book, my prayer is that the Holy Spirit will speak clearly to your heart concerning worship. Allow the spirit of God to engulf you as you read; let it consume you as you worship.

CHAPTER ONE

Understanding Worship

Many complain about an absence of worship, but unfortunately, we often are not clear on what worship really is. In 1 Chronicles 16:8–13 (NLT), after the sacred chest was brought into Jerusalem, it was placed in the tent David had set up, similar to the modern day tent revivals. Before David sent the people home, he gave each of them a small loaf of bread, some meat, and a handful of raisins. David appointed Levites to serve at the sacred chest. He also appointed the Levites to play music at the tent with various kinds of musical instruments, including small harps, stringed instruments, cymbals, and trumpets. When I read this text, it takes me back to Grandma's small country church in Willisville, Arkansas. 1 Chronicles 16:8–36 is the song of praise that David instructed Asaph and his relatives to sing for the first time.

Asaph and his clan were responsible for the daily worship at the tent. Obededom and his sixty-eight relatives were their assistants. Obededom and Hosah were guards at the tent. Zadok and his relatives were to offer sacrifices at the altar every morning and evening. Heman and Jeduthun were their assistants. Heman and Jeduthun were in charge of blowing trumpets, playing the cymbals, and other kinds of musical instruments to worship God.

The Jeduthun clan worked as guards at Gibeon. Part of the psalm in 1 Chronicles 16:8–22 is mentioned in Psalm 105:1–15. The part of the psalm in Chronicles 16:23-33 is mentioned in Psalm 96:1–13. The part of the psalm in 1 Chronicles 16:34–36 is also mentioned in Psalm 96:1–13.

My prayer is that this chapter will help you gain a better understanding of worship, take a self-examination of how you view worship, and to make a conscious decision to embrace Spiritual and True Worship.

As I try to summarize this chapter and come to a concluding message, I will take an expository approach to understanding worship. In doing so, I will discuss three main points:

a. The Nature of Worship

b. The Manner of Worship

c. The Object of Worship

First, the Nature of Worship (vv. 28–30): an inadequate definition of the nature of worship is subjective feelings or experiences. Worship is not about a feeling or how you feel at the moment, nor does it simply emerge from some sporadic, emotional experience. I label these kinds of worshippers "alka-seltzer Christians" — *Plop, plop; fizz, fizz; Oh what a relief it is.* They are the ones who get excited for the moment but fizz away rapidly. The dictionary definition is: declaring God's worth or expressing His praise. The Biblical definition comes from a word that is translated both "worship" and "bow down" or "make obeisance." (www.truthortradition.com/articles/what-is-true-biblical-worship)

In other words, worship is based on our salvation and reflects the Spirit and Truth of God and His Word. Worship reminds us of our position before God and His worthiness and position above us. Worship is for God's glory, praise, and honor—outward bowing down that reflects inward bowing. Inward bowing is a result of recognizing the greatness of God, the smallness of man, and knowing the difference. Worship is an attitude that recognizes the greatness of God and inwardly bows down as a result. This leads to the second point:

The Manner of Worship (vv. 8–12): There are many ways of doing this. Verse 8 has three parts: we are to express gratitude to Him (v. 8a); we pray to

Him (v. 8b), regardless of whether we stand, sit, kneel, or bow—God simply wants us to have a conversation with Him; and we should testify to what He has done for us (v. 8c). When we do Praise and Worship, it is one way of expressing our gratitude to God and a testament for what He has done for us. Although praise is not the same as worship, praise is certainly a part of worship. We see this demonstrated in verses 9a and 9b. Sing to Him and about Him; talk of His wondrous works. David was a praiser. David was a worshipper of God throughout his Palmitic writing—we constantly see it.

a. Oh, make a joyful noise unto the Lord.

b. I was glad when they said unto me … let us go into the house of the Lord.

c. Let everything that has breath, Praise the Lord.

Verse 11 also suggests a manner of worship by prayer. Call on Him in every time of need. We ought to call on Him and seek His face at all times, but there is nothing wrong with calling on Him in times of need. He is the one who said, "Make your requests known."

The Object of Worship (vv. 14–22): He is God. Not only is He God, He is a living God. He is a powerful God (He created the heavens and earth). He is a personal God. I know He is personal because He is an active God; His mercies are new every day. I do not lose sleep at night because of what the world is doing because vs.14 reminds me His judgments are being worked out in the earth. Since worship is an internal attitude, it is expected to show in certain attitudes and actions based on it. When we truly "understand worship," it would include praising the Lord. It would include rejoicing in the Lord; it would include submission to the Lord. It would include obedience to the Lord's Word; it would include reverence of the Lord's person. It would include witnessing for Him, the best way to share His greatness with others. And yes, it would include praying to Him. These all show an important side of worship. They should occur as part of a service. However, when you truly "understand worship," these cannot be limited to a Sunday morning service. It actually becomes a way of life.

Worship is surely missing in modern Christianity. Biblical worship actually permeates all of life. Biblical worship is an attitude that would change the way we think and also the way we live. *"In all thy getting, get understanding."* (Proverbs 7:4) I don't know about you, but I had to seek the Lord earnestly for myself, asking Him to help me understand worship. Asking Him to show me how to worship Him revealed to me the importance of worshipping Him in Spirit and in Truth. I had to ask God to create in me the right attitude of worship. When we are prepared for worship, when there is "a call to worship," your mind and spirit can be wrapped around worship. Knowing the only way your mind and spirit can be wrapped around worship is if you have an attitude of worship. When we have the right attitude for worship, it is then we can worship in Spirit and Truth.

CHAPTER TWO

Preparing for Worship

When you read the Old Testament, you cannot help but see the importance of worship in the lives of the people of God. Abraham worshipped (Genesis 22:5); Jacob worshiped (Hebrews 11:21); Moses worshiped (Exodus 34:8); Joshua worshiped (Joshua 5:14); David worshiped (2 Samuel 12:20), and a host of others.

Worship is an integral part of the lives of the believer. The first commandment is, "*You shall not make for yourself an image in the form of anything in heaven above or on the earth beneath or in the waters below. You shall not bow down to them or worship them; for I, the LORD your God, am a jealous God...*" The fourth commandment is the command to keep the Sabbath as a day of rest and worship. So from the beginning of time, God made it clear that we are to worship Him and worship Him only. And woven into the fabric of creation is a specific day of worship. We find in the New Testament that worship is just as important. The disciples worshiped the Lord (Matt. 28:9), and the New Testament church worshiped regularly (Phil. 3:3). And each time we get a glimpse into heaven, we see worship happening, "*the twenty-four elders fall down before him who sits on the throne and worship him who lives for ever and ever.*" (Rev. 4:10) And at the end of time when God completes His plan of salvation, worship will be all there is as we live in God's presence. Hallelujah. And if you can't worship Him down here, when it is just a rehearsal for up there, how do you expect to be ready? So our highest priority as Christians is to give glory to God, to exalt

Him by giving Him worship. We are created and called to worship: that is the reason we gather every Sunday. But here is what I want to convey as I attempt to bring you, the reader, to a better understanding of worship: our worship should begin long before we enter the sanctuary. That is the mistake too many Christians make because they arrive thinking that worship begins when the service starts or when they arrive. It is also the reason why so many have worship experiences that fall far short of what God intends for us in worship. The bottom line is, we come unprepared. One definition of worship is "our response both personal and corporate to God for who He is and for what He has done, expressed in and by the things we say and the way we live." Merriam-Webster's Collegiate Dictionary (11th ed) defines worship as "reverence offered a divine being." This definition then requires us to reverence God. In scripture, the Hebrew word for worship is *shachah*, meaning "to kneel, stoop, prostrate oneself, or throw oneself down in reverence. This word is closely related to the Hebrew word *yadah,* "to worship with uplifted hands." In the Greek, the word for worship, *proskuneo,* means to express deep respect or adoration by kissing—with words, or by bowing down.

When we prepare for Praise and Worship, we praise God for what He has done, and we worship Him for who He is. You cannot give and experience great worship corporately on Sunday morning without having individually worshiped Him through the week. Corporate worship is important, but it hinges upon our individual worship. And the devil knows that if he can distract us from individual worship, it will hinder our corporate worship. It will impact how we approach worship on Sunday morning.

So how do you prepare for worship? Psalm 24:1–10 is believed by most scholars to have been written not long after David had captured the city of Jerusalem. David's desire was to build a religious and political center for his kingdom in the city of Jerusalem, a permanent place of worship for God. So David brings the Ark of the Covenant to Jerusalem, sets it upon Mount Zion, and asks, "Who can ascend to the hill of the Lord?" to worship. Who can meet with God? Who can come before him in worship? In other words, what makes us worthy and ready to approach God and worship Him? The Scriptures makes clear that to come before God demands one be prepared.

What we find is that there are four keys to personal worship.

1. Take personal responsibility to arrive ready and prepared to worship God.
2. Make the time to spend with God.
3. Worship Him.
4. Pray.

First and foremost, you have to take personal responsibility to arrive ready and prepared to worship God. That means you have to become intentional about developing an intimate relationship with God, which begins with your commitment to worship Him outside of Sunday morning. It is God's desire to always be close to His children. It is His desire to be worshiped by you personally. No one can improve your worship other than you. You can't just show up on Sunday morning and start worshiping. If you do, your worship will never reach its potential. And so, you come to worship cold and unprepared, and it takes time for you to get warmed up and in the right frame of mind. The choir can't just rehearse one night a week and think their singing is all there is to worship. No, you've got to have some personal meditation time. You must have alone time with the Master. You must take some time for prayer and fasting. Then and only then can you enter His gates with thanksgiving and into His courts with praise. I think about when I used to drive a '67 Chrysler New Yorker to school and how it had to be warmed up before driving; if not, it would cut off. And if the engine cut off while driving, the steering wheel would lock up. One morning I was late for school so I neglected to allow the car to warm up before driving off. Low and behold, as I approached a stop sign with a deep bayou-like ditch across from it, the car engine cut off. I went straight through the stop sign into the deep ditch. Surely, I would be late now!

My point of sharing my story is to remind and also to encourage you to understand the importance of having already made spiritual preparation prior to worship; if not, you risk your spiritual engine shutting down, causing you to crash into the deep ditches of despair. That is exactly what happens when we come to worship unprepared. It takes forever to warm up our hearts to focus our minds and free our spirit so that we can enter worship prepared to encounter and honor and glorify the King. Instead, some of us, because we're unprepared, experience our spiritual steering wheel locking up, and we drift off into unwanted places. If we don't take the time to prepare before worship and to worship individually throughout the week, then it takes most of the praise time to get to a place to worship God our Creator and Redeemer. And some of us never even get to that place, and then we walk out of the service saying, "that wasn't a very good service today," when in reality, the worship to God was very good, you just never got your engine warmed up. Worship is both personal and corporate, and there's something unique when you are in the presence of a group of people who have taken responsibility to prepare for worship.

Secondly, you have to make the time to spend with God. The reality is that very few of us have extra time on our hands. But our tendency is if we are going to step up and spend time with God, worshiping Him and developing our relationship with Him, we try to squeeze God into our lives. News Flash: that doesn't cut it. You can't just keep adding things into your life. You've got to choose and prioritize. In other words, you've got to give something up. If you don't spend time with God or anyone else, you will never develop your relationship with Him. You can't just come and spend time with God for one hour on Sunday morning or whatever day your worship is scheduled. It has to be more than that. If this is the only time you read the Word, the only time you pray, the only time you sing praise to God—if this is the only time you worship, then you are in trouble. If you want to get closer to God, He's got to be at the center of your life. Make a kingdom impact; be salt and light in the world and offer your life as an offering for Him, which impacts not only the lives of others but their eternal destiny. Then you've got to spend time in worship of Him daily.

This brings me to the third point. Worship Him. Personal worship can take many forms. There are some worship practices which can not only draw you closer to God, but can lead you into greater and deeper worship of Him.

One worship practice is to reflect on what God is doing in your life—how He has blessed you, guided you, and how He has corrected you. Think about the opportunities He has opened for you. Too often we go through life at warp speed, and we fail to see and acknowledge that God has been moving in our lives. Another worship practice is to reflect on the sacrifice of Christ on the cross. We often speak of what Jesus did for us on the cross. We acknowledge it through wearing crosses, singing about it, adorning our churches, and sometimes even our homes with crosses. But do you ever take the time to really consider the magnitude of the fact that Jesus went to the cross for your sins personally? And that He who was sinless took on your sins, was whipped, beaten, mocked, scorned, and eventually hung on a cross, which slowly suffocated Him to death over a period of several hours. Some worship practices we easily neglect are: praying, reading and studying His Word, and taking full advantage of praise and worship.

Lastly, you have got to pray. The Bible says, "*Don't worry about anything, but in everything, by prayer, present your requests to God and the peace of God which surpasses all understanding will guard your hearts and minds in Christ Jesus.*" (Philippians 4:6) The Bible also says, "*Man ought to always pray, pray without ceasing.*" (Luke 18:1; 1 Thessalonians 5:17) But once you pray, Colossians 3:23 encourages us, "*Whatever you do, work at it with all your heart, as working for the Lord, not for men.*" And then, "*Always be prepared to give an answer to everyone who asks you to give the reason for the hope you have.*" (1 Peter 3:15) But do it with gentleness and respect. Jesus called us to be servants, and His last words to us were to make disciples. This reminds us that all of life is our worship of God as we make our bodies a living sacrifice, holy and acceptable to God. If you want to be empowered and prepared for worship, do it because you saw God move in your life during the week as you served others and shared the Good News with them. If you want to know how to prepare for worship, you've got to yield to God's will, and each day offer yourself to God and His plan for your life. If you want to know how to prepare for worship, surrender to Him no matter the call and no matter the sacrifice. If you want to know how to prepare for worship, when you wake up in the mornings, lift your eyes towards heaven and say, "Father I stretch my hands to Thee; no other help I know, if Thou withdraw Thyself from me." You've got to get up early and listen for the Master's voice, saying, "Let everything that have breath praise the Lord." And as you walk into your place of worship, wherever it may be, walk in saying, "I was glad when they said unto me, let us go into the house of the Lord." You've got to open your mouth like Peter, who in his moment of excitement said, "Lord, it's just good for us to be here." (Matthew 17:4)

CHAPTER THREE

A Call to Worship

In many churches our time of worship begins with a *Call to Worship.* The substance of what occurs during that time varies. Sometimes the choir will sing; occasionally there will be a special praise song presented. What is important to know is that everything from the *Call to Worship* to the *Benediction* is a part of worship. Reading announcements or recognitions, and yes, even tithes and offerings, are included in our worship experience. Please understand this is why there must be order during the entire worship. The call to worship signifies to all in attendance that we have come to worship and now is when we start.

In the book of Psalms, we find another call to worship, though not necessarily presented as a time to worship but rather as an opportunity to do so. Through the Psalmist, God issues an invitation for us to worship Him.

Who is to worship God?

The call to worship is to simply *come.* This is an exhortation to assemble or congregate for the purpose of worship. The call goes out to the people of God—to us. The text states, "let us come." The place of worship to which we are invited to come is into the very presence of God. Psalms 95:2 says to come before His presence; the Psalmist is direct and inclusive. This invitation encourages us to begin with singing or rejoicing. Not only are we to "sing and make melody in our hearts" as Paul had encouraged the church at Ephesus to do, but the second part of the verses of Psalms 95:1–2 shows that such singing and rejoicing is to be expressed aloud. When the religious leaders asked Jesus to silence His followers who lauded Him with praise and adoration at His entrance into Jerusalem, His response was, *"I tell you if these become silent, the stones will cry out."* (Luke 19:40) As the church of the living God, we have the privilege of praise and worship, and we must not be content to allow the rocks to cry out or be satisfied to give our opportunity to others. For those of us who know Jesus as our Savior, no one else can or should praise Him in our stead.

Worship format is so much of a discussion and even debated today in religious circles. Everyone's style of worship is different. While some may simply lift their hands in adoration to God, others will lay prostrate before the Lord in worship. In these verses, the Psalmist mentions at least one other reason for praising the Lord. Not only are we to sing *joyfully*, but we are to sing aloud *thankfully*. Our expressions of praise and rejoicing should be with joy and thanksgiving, and they should be done enthusiastically as evidenced by the repeated call to "shout" to the Lord.

There are three reasons we worship our God. We worship God because:

1. Our God is awesome.

2. Our God is worthy of worship.

3. Our God is personal.

Our God is Awesome. (Psalms 95:3–5) As if joy and thanksgiving were not enough, David moves on with an even more compelling reason to *sing, praise,* and *shout* unto God. And it is simply, "He is an awesome God."

When Rich Mullins penned the song *Our God is an Awesome God*, obviously he experienced the awesomeness of God. He wrote: *Our God is an awesome God, He reigns from heaven above, with wisdom, power, and love, our God is an awesome God.*

First, He is a great God. His magnitude as God is awesome. He is extreme, vast, magnificent, and so much more that makes him indescribable. As if being a great God were not enough, He is also a great King. This speaks of His rule and reign as King as well as His kingdom. The Psalmist seems to have no other word to appropriately describe His Godhead and Kingship beyond *great.*

Second, He is the owner of everything from the deepest valleys to the highest hills—all the land and all the sea. To say that He holds it in His hands speaks of the greatness of our God. Even little children are taught, *He's got the whole world in His hand. He's got the itty bitty baby in His hands.*

Third, He is the Creator of all that is. The knowledge that all that we have and all that is around us is from a *Great God and King.* (Psalms 95:5)

Our God is worthy of worship. (Psalms 95:6) The overflow of joy and thanksgiving in shouts of song and praise, along with the realization of the awesomeness of God must culminate in worship. To come into His presence and not worship Him is a contradiction of ideas. To the Hebrews, the idea of worship was synonymous with bowing down before the object of adoration. Therefore, we are instructed to kneel down before the Lord. Why would we kneel before Him? Because we are overcome with joy, gratitude, and awe, and He is greater than we are. Kneeling before Him shows our submissive attitude and spirit before this *great God* whom we serve. We don't kneel much in the twenty-first century. The spirit of the self-made person is alive and well. Today's philosophy is to get as much power as possible and submit to no authority. The lack of respect for authority is prevalent. Children don't respect their parents; students don't respect their teachers, and employees don't respect their employers. Yet we live in a world where many still believe one should respect the position if not the person. We live in a time when some leaders at the highest level of leadership do not seem to respect their own position, making it quite difficult to hold others to a higher standard of expectation. Respect for the things of our God is on the decline. Our God is worthy to be worshiped because He is so much greater than we are.

Our God is personal. (Psalms 95:7) He is worthy to be worshipped because He is a personal God. Though He is the God of many, He is able to be the God of one. That means He knows each of us, and we know Him. Such a relationship has been His intent and plan from the beginning. His desire for man is evident through the entire Old Testament—revealed in the Gospels, refined in the Epistles, and rejoiced over in the Revelation.

God desires to be our God, and we are to be His people. This theme, sewn into the fabric of Holy Scripture, will come to pass according to Revelation 21:3. *"And I heard a great voice out of heaven saying, Behold, the tabernacle of God is with men, and he will dwell with them, and they shall be his people, and God himself shall be with them, and be their God."* The redeemed of the Lord worship because we understand that we are already the people of His pasture, and He is our God. True worshipers are eagerly looking forward to that time when we are gathered to Him to dwell in His presence forever. Our Lord is to be worshiped for He alone is worthy. When we talk about Sunday service, in many churches we often refer to the overall event as the *worship service.* We either consciously or subconsciously divide it into two parts.

Let me explain. For example, at the church where I serve as servant leader, the Savannah Missionary Baptist Church in Fayetteville, North Carolina, we have someone considered as the *worship leader,* who provides direction to all the events leading up to the message, which is brought by someone called the *preacher.* The process of coming together, giving expression to our joy and thanksgiving, seeing God's awesomeness and realizing His great love for us ultimately leads us to being receptive to hearing His voice. Hearing His voice, which comes from the proclamation of the Word, is an essential part of the worship experience. Without hearing the Word proclaimed, we may become like the children of Israel in the wilderness, who demonstrated faithlessness. We know that "*faith comes by hearing and hearing by the word of God.*" (Romans 10:17) It is spiritually dangerous to come to worship service Sunday after Sunday and not listen and hear the proclamation of the Word. The consequence of unbelief would be that we would not heed the call to worship.

Lastly, there is a warning to those who do not worship God or heed the call to worship. Looking over the Psalmist's shoulder into the past, he remembered that the children of Israel in Exodus 17:7 had unacceptable behavior in the sight of the Lord. Notice that the worshippers in that text are admonished not to harden their heart. The examples of Meribah and Massah are cited. These were two places where the children of Israel hardened their hearts against the Lord. They tested and tried Him. Interestingly, the text states that they did so even *though they had seen my work.* Their lack of trust and challenge of His ability and power were offered even after seeing His miraculous works. One could hardly fathom questioning and rebelling against the God who brought His children through the Red Sea on dry ground. How would anyone question and doubt a God with that much power? This leaves room for a personal question: how many "Red Seas" has that same God parted in your life? Isn't that like some of us? God has been good to us. As Grandma would say, "He has brought us out of this and that and even healed our bodies," yet we come to church or to the worship setting acting as if God has never done anything for us. Failing to worship God and choosing rather to question and rebel against Him is not acceptable and is the very thing the Psalmist warns against. I pray that each reader of this book now knows and understands the consequences of failing to worship our great God because it is a Call to Worship.

Failing to recognize and follow God's way is a sure recipe for sin. In order to follow His ways, we must spend time getting to know Him. A rebellious spirit will hinder that endeavor. How many times do we miss the opportunities of rest in Jesus because we are rebellious in Spirit? A true worshiper of God is more concerned with worshipping a Holy God than promoting their personal agenda. A true worshiper understands that God indeed knows the thoughts of man. Worship is not merely some given action to be performed. Worship is heartfelt and genuinely offered to a holy and omniscient God. True worship is not birthed out of compulsion, but rather out of privilege. Worshiping God should be from the joy in our hearts because of His salvation. He has done great and mighty things for us, and our worship of Him should be from a heart of thanksgiving for all that He has done. Worshiping Him with joy and thanksgiving is how we are to worship.

The text does not mention worshiping with hymns or praise choruses. Too many churches are more concerned with how to worship Him and often forfeit the opportunity to worship. God is not concerned with whether we use hymns, praise songs, or instruments to praise Him. The call is simply to worship him. A Call to Worship includes laying aside our personal desires, preferences, and plans and picking up the attitude of praise. The Psalmist declares in this psalm, *O come, let us worship and bow down, let us kneel before the Lord our Maker* [in reverent praise and supplication] (Psalm 95:6). The next time you are in a worship environment, don't wait on others to worship; be the example of a true worshipper who understands the Call to Worship.

CHAPTER FOUR

Attitudes of Worship

I discussed a Call to Worship in chapter three. We discovered that our God is awesome; our God is worthy of worship, and our God is personal. We saw how God is good in His choice and care for us, and that He is great in His creation and control of all. We concluded that if you come to church in response to anything other than to God's goodness and God's greatness, you have only come to church. But if you come to church in response to God's goodness and to His greatness, you have come to worship.

In chapter two we learned to properly prepare for worship.

- One must take personal responsibility to arrive ready and prepared to worship God.
- The worshipper must make time to spend with God.
- Worship Him and make prayer a part of preparation.

There's a huge difference between coming to church and coming to worship. We worship God, first of all, because of who God is: His nature, character and power. God created us to worship Him, and when we don't worship God, we don't cease to worship, we simply worship someone or something else. And worshipping anything or anyone other than our Creator distorts our perspectives and values in life. If we worship possessions, we measure the value of a person based on how much he or she owns. If we worship our work, we measure the value of a person based on his or her abilities. If we worship ourselves, we measure the value of another based on our perception of ourselves. In this chapter, I will discuss the three attitudes needed to worship our Creator and to restore a right relationship with God. Since I will be talking about the attitudes of Worship, let me define what attitude is.

Attitudes are the habits of thinking that eventually direct our words and actions. If we have a positive attitude, we are in the habit of thinking positively, and our words and actions will show this optimism. There are three necessary attitudes of Worship exhibited in the eight verses by the prophet Isaiah in Isaiah 6: 1–8.

Consider the following:

1. The Lordship of God

2. The humility of mankind

3. The servanthood of worshippers

The first attitude of worship is *The Lordship of God.* We see this in verses 1–4. Isaiah served as a prophet of God for a period of time before he saw this vision from God. I believe the reason Isaiah didn't see God's majesty and glory before this time was because Isaiah wrongly placed his confidence and allegiance in King Uzziah's reign. But now the human king is dead. Sometimes it takes God removing people and things from our lives before we can see Him for who He is. It may help if I give you some background. King Uzziah ruled Judah with great prosperity and victory for fifty-two years. He began his reign humbly and earnestly seeking God, but as time went on, King Uzziah became prideful. His arrogance led to a final act of disregard for God's order, and God struck Uzziah with leprosy, ending his reign. You can read about this in 2 Chronicles 26. The problem with putting our trust in things or people is that we become blind to God's majesty, glory, power, wisdom, and resources that are infinitely more valuable and pure. And when we don't see God as He is, we won't worship Him as He deserves. In order to worship God as He deserves, we need to possess the attitude of the lordship of God. Jesus said in Matthew 6:24, "*No one can serve two masters, either he will hate the one and love the other, or he will be devoted to the one and despise the other. You cannot serve both God and money*" (or materialism). The one who controls our thoughts, emotions, actions, and our time is our Lord and the one we worship. If God is not the Lord of all, He is not the Lord at all.

My question to you is, who controls your time? Do television programs control your time? Does sleep control your time? Do hobbies control your time? Do your fears control your time? Ephesians 5:15 says, "*Be very careful, then, how you live—not as unwise but as wise, making the most of every opportunity.*" Some of us will scream out against the lordship of God in our lives because they don't want God telling them what to do. They want to be their own boss. Too often we want to blend in with the rest of the world; we want to live an "I do *me* lifestyle." You may come to church, but you are not coming to worship unless you come with the attitude of giving control of your life to God. So, the first attitude of worship is the Lordship of God.

The second attitude of worship is the Humility of Mankind. We see this in verses 5–7. When Isaiah saw God, he not only recognized that God was the true Ruler of his life, but he also recognized his own sinfulness and the sinfulness of the people. Humility is the ability to see ourselves as God sees us. Believers must stop going along with what the world is doing, trying to please man. It is much better to please God. The *"I'm gonna do it my way"* attitude across America wrongly reacts against the Bible's evaluation of mankind. This kind of attitude leads one to believe, "This is my life; I do want I want," or "This is my body; I do with it as I please." That is far from the Truth that my Bible tells me: "*Know ye that the LORD he is God: it is he that hath made us, and not we ourselves;*" (Psalm 100: 3). After King Uzziah died, Isaiah saw God, and he realized he had made a tragic mistake by praising Uzziah instead of praising God and by placing his trust in Uzziah instead of in God. So Isaiah confessed his sin and received God's solution that he needed—live coals to cleanse his lips, to remove his guilt and atone for his sin. Without humility, mankind lives in denial of his own sinfulness, or mankind will live with useless attempts to salvage his own sinfulness.

Only with humility can we admit our sinfulness and receive God's solution. Well, you may ask, how does humility tie into the worship of God? Do you not know that the religions of the world are not really a worship of other gods? Religions of the world are really a worship of self-effort to please or to appease fears, guilt, and maybe God. Christianity, on the other hand, requires humility to confess our inability to salvage ourselves, so we receive God's solution in Jesus's death on the cross. The humility of mankind allows the rightful Ruler, God, to take His place. Arrogance hinders the worship of God; humility fosters the worship of God.

The first attitude of worship is the Lordship of God; the second attitude of worship is the Humility of Mankind, and the third attitude of worship is the Servanthood of Worshippers, verses 2–3 and verse 8. While Isaiah and the seraphs are quite different, the things that are in common are their worship of God and their servanthood to God. Seraphs are angelic beings that have six wings. As with all angelic beings, their purposes are to worship and serve God. The similarities between Isaiah and the seraphs are quite astonishing. As with Isaiah's servant response, we see the seraphs' servant response follows only after their reverence for God and their humility before God. The two wings that cover their faces demonstrate reverence for God. The two wings that cover their feet demonstrate humility before God. With the two remaining wings, the seraphs carried out the orders of God. Mankind's service to God without first possessing the lordship of God and the humility of mankind will always be blindly covered by selfish ambitions. One way to demonstrate the Servanthood Attitude that ties into worship is to determine whether in your own time of reading the Bible and prayer or in your Sunday gathering that you are coming with the habit of thought that God is Lord. Shake off other things and people from their influence on you. Say to yourself and to God, "God, You are my Lord. You give the orders. I won't let the philosophies from our culture - I won't let my fears - I won't let my lusts for things set my priorities. You are my Lord, and I am Your servant. Lord, I will obey." When you enter God's presence with the attitudes of the Lordship of God, the Humility of Mankind, and the

Servanthood of a Worshipper, God will show Himself to you and speak to you with such clarity that you will be able to identify with Isaiah's vision, and you too will be given the opportunity to respond in service to God.

In Vernon Whaley's book *Call to Worship,* he speaks of Worship Wars, which are all about our attitude. He points out that the first misguided worship begins in the heart. Keep in mind what's in our heart drives or motivates our attitude. Whaley goes on to say that the very first seed of misguided worship sprouted in the heart of Satan. He says: "Satan wanted to bring down the Creator of the cosmos and end all worship of Him in heaven." But his efforts failed miserably. I share this because people need to be warned—that when you truly worship God, Satan's attack against you and those you love will possibly become relentless. Not only am I warning you, but I aim to encourage you with God's Word from this same author, Isaiah, that *No weapon that is formed against you, shall prosper.* (Isaiah 54:17) Before we can truly be God's servants, we must humbly choose God to be our Master. The attitudes of the Lordship of God, the Humility of Mankind, and the Servanthood of Worshippers are not chosen just on Sunday mornings. This choice must be made morning after morning until it becomes the habit of our thinking. So the next time you attend worship service, arrive with the right attitude of Worship; go with the right attitude about who God is. Go with the right attitude about what God has done for you, and don't be afraid to worship Him, knowing that the true Worshipper must worship God in Spirit and in Truth. When you worship God in Spirit and in Truth, you won't mind giving Him praise; you won't mind saying, *Oh taste and see that the Lord is good.* (Psalm 34:8) With the right attitude, you don't mind saying, *Oh magnify the Lord with me, let us exalt His name together.* (Psalm 34:3) With the right attitude towards worship, you don't mind saying, *Worship the Lord in the beauty of His holiness.*

CHAPTER FIVE

Spiritual Worship

In his epilogue of his first letter, John summarizes the conclusions of the epistle in a series of three certainties:

1. Sin is a threat to fellowship, and it should be regarded as foreign to the believer's position in Christ.

2. The believer stands with God against the satanic world system.

3. The incarnation produces true knowledge and communion with Christ.

In this epistle, John speaks not to any particular church, but to all the Christians of that age, and, more specifically, to them with whom he resided. Keep in mind that this was not a sent letter; rather, he read his letter, probably because he was not able to preach to them any longer due to his extreme old age, for he was present with those to whom it was more immediately intended. He does not talk directly of faith, which Paul had done; nor of inward and outward holiness, of which Paul, James, and Peter had spoken, but of the foundation of all, as well as speaking of the Holy Communion, which the faithful have with God the Father, Son, and Holy Ghost.

In the preface he describes the authority by which he wrote and spoke (1 John 1:1–4) and expressly points out the design of his present writing. The recapitulation begins in verse 1: *We know that he who is born of God,* who sees and loves God, *sinneth not,* (1 John 5:18) so long as this loving faith abideth in him. *We know we are of God* (1 John 5:19*)*, children of God, by the witness and the fruit of the Spirit; *and the whole world,* all who have not the Spirit, *lieth in the wicked one.* (1 John 5:19) *We know that the Son of God is come, and hath given us* [a spiritual] *understanding, that we may know the true One,* [the faithful and true witness]. *And we are in the true One, this is the true God, and eternal life* (1 John 5:20).

If we are admonished to "worship in Spirit and in Truth," I want to take some time to talk about both Spiritual Worship and True Worship. To fully understand what it means to worship God in Spirit and in Truth, we must first look at the meaning behind both of these words. Spirit in the Greek is *pneuma.* It is where we get the word "pneumatic," which means air, essence, soul, or principle. Jesus addresses the issue of worship first with the unseen—God, soul, principles. Worshipping God in spirit is to worship Him in our inner man (the unseen part of us, our spirit, where our principles are).

According to Mark 12:30 Jesus tells us to *Love the Lord your God with all your heart, with all your soul, with all your mind, and with all your strength.* Heart, soul, and mind are words directly related to worshipping (loving) God in Spirit. The word Truth in the Greek is *aletheia*; it is important to know that the Gospel of John often equates *alethia* to Jesus. Truth is also often equated to the Word of God. John 1:1 says, "In the beginning was the Word, and the Word was with God, and the Word was God." Therefore, the Word (truth) is God. Did Jesus not say *"I am the way, the Truth, and the life"*? So, if *pneuma* spirit, means inner, it is equally important to know the Greek word *sarx,* which is for flesh; it means the external body, the natural man. Jesus addresses the issue of worship secondly with what is seen—external body or actions. Worshipping God in Truth is to worship Him in our outer man through our actions. Again, Mark 12:30 Jesus tells us to *Love the Lord your God with all your heart, with all your soul, with all your mind, and with all your strength.* Strength is a word directly related to worshipping God in Truth (through action). Jesus Christ tells us in John 4 to worship the Father in spirit and in truth so we may understand the principles and action at work behind our worship.

Four characteristics of worshipping God in Spirit and Truth:

1. Reverence

2. Adoration

3. Humility

4. Obedience

1. Reverence: We worship God in Spirit though reverence. Reverence is defined as *feelings of deep respect or devotion.* We know David to be a praiser and a worshipper, listen to him in Psalm 5:7: *But as for me, I will come* (in other words, choose to come) *into Your house* (for devotion*) in the multitude of Your mercy; In fear* (deep awe) *of You* (indicating respect for Yahweh*). I will worship toward Your holy temple."* To worship God in spirit, our attitudes and principles must reflect the characteristics of reverence.

2. Adoration: We worship God in Spirit though adoration. *I love the Lord, because He has heard my voice and my supplications.* (Psalm 116:1) Remember, we praise God for what He has done; however, when we worship God in spirit, our attitudes and principles reflect the characteristics of adoration. Adoration for God, or to adore Him, is a desire to praise God, but it is only the beginning point; you must then move to developing a lifestyle of praise. You should strive to adore God on a daily basis. This is not something that will come easily; you must work it. A life of overflowing praise requires commitment and work. God is worthy to be adored, and it will produce significant benefits in your walk with Him. I'm sure this sounds good, and you want to adore God in such a way that your walk will be closer with Him, so much so that your whole life may be impacted spiritually.

But maybe you're not sure how to do it. Well, let me help you. If you apply the following to your worship, I believe it will help you.

a. Make the commitment to adore God. The Psalmist declares his commitment in Psalm 71:6: *By You I have been upheld from birth; You are He who took me out of my mother's womb. My praise shall be continually of You.* You've got to determine in your heart that you will adore God daily, in all the circumstances of life.

b. Saturate yourself with God's Word. The Word of God fuels a lifestyle of adoration. Your knowledge of God will determine the depth of your praise to Him. The Word of God says, *I will praise you with uprightness of heart, when I learn your righteous judgments.* (Psalm 119:7) As your knowledge of God and His ways increase, your adoration of Him will grow deeper and more intimate.

c. Then ask God to teach you how to praise Him. Develop a vocabulary of praise. Believers often do not praise God because they do not know what to say. There is an important need to grow in your understanding of Him. You can develop a vocabulary of praise by studying His characteristics, His names, His pictures, and His titles in the Scripture. Such as: "You are El Shaddi; You are Jehovah Nissi; You are Wonderful Counselor." You've got to know who He is. Turn every truth you learn about God into praise as you grow in your knowledge of who God is; use those truths to adore Him.

d. Then you've got to meditate on God on His throne. (Revelation 4–5) As you meditate on God on His throne, it prepares you to praise Him. It will help you remember whose presence you are entering. It can also strengthen your desire to praise Him.

3. Humility is the third characteristic. We worship God in Truth though humility. Humility is the act of realizing that we are not in control—that God is—and submitting to His will for our life. God says in Isaiah 55:9, *For as the heavens are higher than the earth, so are my ways higher than your ways, and my thoughts than your thoughts.* Satan had it made in heaven before he got beside himself. He was the minister of music, but selfish motives crept in. In order for us to worship God in truth, our actions must reflect the characteristics of humility. There are far too many who profess the name of the Lord and want to do it their way. They'd much rather someone bow down to them than bow to Christ Jesus.

4. Obedience. We worship God in Truth though obedience. Obedience is holding true the commandments of God, and abiding in His will and plans for us. We can reflect on 1 Samuel 15:22–23: *Behold, to obey is better than sacrifice, and to hearken than the fat of rams. For rebellion is as the sin of witchcraft, and stubbornness is as iniquity and idolatry.* To worship God in truth, our actions must reflect the characteristics of obedience. Having the right attitude when we worship God is a critical part of our relationship with Him. God wants us to enjoy Him, and if any wrong ideas or motives exist in our life, then we have barriers that are keeping us from the fullness of what God has for us. Maybe you see that you lack in one of these areas. Perhaps you are good at talking the talk, but not walking the walk. Maybe, just maybe, you've been an apple on Sunday, and morphed into a banana on Monday. If that's you, God allows us the opportunity to repent and come to Him. For His Word says, "I am spirit," and "the True worshipper must worship me in Spirit and in Truth." This can only happen when we crucify the flesh. When we put self aside and concentrate on the Master, our walk will be the same daily. The wiles of the enemy will have a difficult time derailing our godly characteristics. Our true godly self leads us to worship God as El Shaddai. We can worship Him as Jehovah Jireh because we know He is our Provider. We worship Him as Jehovah Shalom because when all hell is breaking out around us, He gives us Peace. It is a wonderful thing to know that when the doctors diagnose us with a dreaded disease, we can still worship Him as Jehovah Rapha. God is still our Healer.

CHAPTER SIX

True Worship

When talking about True Worship, one must first identify what is the priority of Worship. Worship is not the slow song that the choir sings; worship is not the amount you place in the offering basket, and worship is not volunteering in children's church. Yes, these may be acts or expressions of worship, but they do not define what true worship really is. There are numerous definitions of the word *worship*, yet one in particular encapsulates the priority we should give to worship as a spiritual discipline: Worship is "to honor with extravagant love and extreme submission" (Webster's Dictionary,1828). True worship, in other words, is defined by the priority we place on who God is in our lives and where God is on our list of priorities. True worship is a matter of the heart expressed through a lifestyle of holiness. Thus, if your lifestyle does not express the beauty of holiness through an extravagant or exaggerated love for God, and you do not live in extreme or excessive submission to God, then I invite you to make worship a non-negotiable priority in your life. We worship God because He is God—period. Our extravagant love and extreme submission to the Holy One flows out of the reality that God loved us first. It is highly appropriate to thank God for all the things He has done for us. However, True Worship is shallow if it is solely an acknowledgement of God's wealth. Psalm 96:5-6 says, *For all the gods of the nations are idols, but the Lord made the heavens. Splendor and majesty are before him; strength and glory are in his sanctuary.* In other words, our worship must be toward the one who is worthy simply because of His identity as the Omnipotent, Omniscient, and Omnipresent One, and not just because God is wealthy and able to meet our needs and answer our prayers. We must focus our practice of worship on the worthiness of God and not His wealthiness.

Charles Spurgeon delivered a sermon in 1915 at the Metropolitan Tabernacle, Newington, dealing with this very topic, stating that even in the Christian Church we have great diversities of opinion as to what is the true form of worship. Some are for the quietude of a Friends' meeting-house; some are for the stormy music of the cathedral. Some will have it that God is best praised in silence; others that he is best honored with flute, harp, psaltery, and all kinds of music. Is it so difficult, then, to know what kind of worship God will accept? It is very difficult if it be left to the guesses of man; it is not at all difficult if we turn to the Word of God. There we shall find great room for diversities of mode, but we shall find ourselves shut up by a consecrated intolerance to a few matters of spirit.

In chapter five we discovered that worshipping God in spirit is to worship Him in our inner man (the unseen part of us, our spirit, where our principles are.) This chapter's supporting scripture takes us to Jacob's well where Jesus and the Samaritan woman discussed the matter of worship. We know from the history of the text that Samaritans and Jews differed as to where one should worship. Samaritans believed they should worship on Mt. Geranium. Some history on Mt. Geranium reveals that Josephus gives the following account of the erection of this temple: Manasseh, brother of Jaddua, the high priest, was threatened by the Jews with deprivation of his priestly office because of a marriage he had contracted with a foreign woman. His father-in-law, Sanballat, obtained permission from Alexander the Great, then besieging Tyre, to build a temple on Mount Gerizim. Manasseh was its first high priest. It became the refuge of all Jews who had violated the precepts of the Mosaic Law. The establishment of the counterfeit worship on Gerizim embittered and perpetuated the schism between the Jews and the Samaritans. So because of this, Jews understood that true worship should be in Jerusalem. Jesus said the time was coming for a different kind of worship where worship would not be defined by its location where true worshippers would worship the Father in spirit and truth.

What does it mean to worship the Father in spirit and truth? Many say it means:

a. To worship God from the heart ("in spirit") or pneuma (New-ma)

b. To worship God as He directs us in His Word to worship ("in truth")

Note the contrast made by Jesus. The Jews had worshipped correctly by going to Jerusalem, but the time was coming when place would not be important. A contrast is being made between Old Testament worship and New Testament worship. Somehow, Old Testament worship had not been "in spirit and truth." Yet God required worship from the heart from the Jews, (Deut 6:4-7; Isaiah 1:10-18) when God rebuked their sacrifices, offerings, and their worship. If "in spirit and truth" does not mean "from the heart and in harmony with God's Word", then what does it mean?

Since we've dealt with the Spirit part, let's look at the Truth part of worship.

Worshipping God in Truth means to offer *True (Real) Worship*

Does this mean to worship according to the commands of God? Certainly we should do this, but this is no contrast to what God expected in the Old Testament in Deut 5:32-33. Jesus admitted that the Jews were right in their worship (John 4:22), so what is the contrast between worship that was and that which "now is"? Don't confuse the difference between true and false worship, but between that which is true (real) and that which had been a shadow. A worship was coming that was more in keeping with truth and reality—now, as opposed to "Shadow (Symbol) Worship." Many elements of worship in the Old Testament were simply a shadow or figure of what was to come. The Tabernacle was a symbol. (Hebrews 9:8-9) The Law with its worship was only a shadow of that to come. Christ is now in the true tabernacle (heaven). (Hebrews 9:11-12,24) We should expect the worship of the true to be different from that of the shadow.

We have already seen that to be the case:

1. Old Covenant worship, which was but a shadow, was physical in nature.

2. New Covenant worship is according to the true realities (God is Spirit, Christ in heaven) and is therefore more spiritual in nature. The emphasis is on that which is true (real), not which was a shadowy symbol of things to come. This explanation of worshipping God "in spirit and truth" is more in keeping with the immediate context. Since God is seeking "true worshippers" who worship Him accordingly (John 4:23), allow me to give some thoughts about our worship today that may be appropriate.

Worshippping God Today.

Not all worship is acceptable. Allow me to explain. There is vain worship, Matt 15:7-9, when Jesus called them hypocrites because they honored Him with their mouth, but their hearts was far from Him. They, like so many today, come to church, i.e., we call ourselves worshipping God based on traditions of men, while ignoring the commands of God. Traditional worship can be offered without involving our "hearts" (spirits).

There are all kinds of worship. There is *ignorant worship*—Acts 17:22-23. They were worshipping an "Unknown God" on Mars Hill. Ignorant worship is being ignorant of the true nature of God, ignorant of the worship He desires.

Then there is *will worship*—Col 2:20-23, self-imposed, not God-directed but what we like, or what we think is good. Just because we worship God, does not mean He is pleased with our worship. But I declare unto you: God seeks True Worshippers, who worship God with their spirits, seeking to engage the spirit (mind) more than the organs of the body. Those who are content with the simplicity of worship that stresses the spiritual side of man, who worship God according to the rule that He hath prescribed, in truth and reality, not desiring to return to the carnal ordinances imposed until a time of reformation. I am referring to those content with the worship ordained in the New Covenant—those who can worship God anywhere, anytime, with true spiritual worship like Paul and Silas in Acts 16:25—even while in jail. It didn't matter because they knew who God was to them. It was right there in a jail cell they praised and worshipped the true and living God.

How can we be sure to offer spiritual and true worship acceptable to God? I'll tell you how: if we'd just look to the New Testament for our authority in worship. Worship in ways ordained by Christ and His apostles. For God is Spirit; our worship should be spiritual and not limited to special places. The emphasis should be on the spiritual (pneuma) and not the physical—not how it looks, not how it sounds, not how it feels. We can be assured according to Scripture that "*the hour is coming, and now is, when the true worshipers will worship the Father in spirit and truth.*" So remember we praise Him for dying on the cross for our sins. We praise Him for bringing us through our trials, struggles, and tribulations. We praise Him for the material things we have. But we worship Him because He is a sovereign God. He's an omnipotent God, an omnipresent God. We worship Him simply because He is the "I AM GOD," and such worship must be in spirit and in truth.

CHAPTER SEVEN

The Meaning of Worship

People attend church for many reasons:

a. Out of tradition

b. Out of a sense of responsibility

c. To see who shows up

You may have experienced an encounter with the person who missed service, and before asking what the message was about, they're asking, "Did so and so show up?" It has been twenty years since the world was on pins and needles talking about the millennium, afraid that computers were going to crash. Some even predicted that it would be Armageddon (the end of the world). I have heard people talking about all sorts of things that they are going to do differently when a New Year comes. Some even make New Year's resolutions (I am not sure what they are resolving). It is amazing to me how people do all kinds of things for the New Year: eat black-eyed peas for good luck, eat greens hoping for more money in the New Year, and after eating all of the black-eyed peas and greens, the only thing that changes in their life is their weight.

The question that has been asked is what are people going to do to change their spiritual life? We walk around talking about new promises for a better life, but what about the promises God has already made? That if we "seek first the Kingdom of God, and His righteousness, all these other things shall be added unto us." (Matthew 6:33 KJV)

In John 4:21-24 the story is told of Jesus leaving Judea, headed to Galilee. It was not by chance that Jesus meets this woman after the disciples had gone away. Jesus needed to be alone with this woman without any distractions. For some, in order to focus on true worship and get to the place God wants you to be, you will need to get away from some of the people you are hanging with. There are even some church folk that you just might have to separate yourself from. Why? Because they are distracting you from True Worship. Distraction during worship is a tool Satan uses. While preaching, pastors can often become distracted by a lot of movement during service. I am personally distracted when the choir behind me is constantly talking to one another during service. But for you, your distraction might be thinking about all of your troubles. You can even be distracted because of an ill attitude that you came to the worship service with.

But God is speaking to all of us. He is looking for the "True Worshippers." Granted, many come to a worship service for no other reason than to worship God in the beauty of His holiness. I encourage the True Worshipper to remain focused in your daily doings, as you go about in your usual avocation. Continue to worship God in Spirit and in Truth. The Greek for Worshipper is *proskynētis*. The center of Jesus's discussion with this woman is similar to everyday discussions among churchgoers. It's about form and styles of worship. Jesus said to her, "You worship and don't know what you worship." (Matthew 4:22) Is that the case for us? Are we worshipping Sunday after Sunday and yet not knowing whom we are worshipping? Allow me to paraphrase verse 23, "You are living in a time and the hour has come, that the True Worshippers will come to church for no other reason than to seek God, praise Him, honor Him and forget about everything else around you." Jesus came to Samaria for a purpose. He came there to transform the life of a woman—one who had been confused, abused, and used. We ought to come for worship for like reasons, if not to transform others but to be transformed ourselves. Here was the root of her problems. Her relationships were wrong. Her reasoning was wrong, and her religion was wrong. Everything about her could have been drastically changed if only her life had been changed by a relationship with the one true God.

Nothing in our lives will ever be totally in order until we get this one thing right: Jesus has got to be the center of our life. Jesus transformed this woman. He changed her life. God wants to change us, and He wants to change the Church for the better—change the focus away from materialism to kingdom building. He wants to transform the way that we worship. We must not rush God in the midst of worshipping Him. And when we worship in spirit and in truth, we then become the True Worshippers.

There are a few things God is looking for in the True Worshipper.

God is seeking those who will worship in the Spirit

God is seeking those who will worship in the Spirit. Phil 3:3 reminds us, "For we are the circumcision, which worship God in the spirit, and rejoice in Christ Jesus, and have no confidence in the flesh." When we worship in the Spirit, the Spirit produces life, and when we come alive spiritually, the services will come alive, and once the services come alive, thanks be to God, the sermons will come alive.

There is a story told of a man in the choir who couldn't sing. Others tried to help him find other places of ministry in the church without hurting his feelings, but to no success. The choir director became so desperate that he went to the pastor. He told the pastor that he had to do something or he would quit, and half the choir would as well. After trying unsuccessfully to beat around the bush and make a point, the pastor finally told the man that he needed to leave the choir. "Why?" asked the man.

The pastor reluctantly said, "Several people have told me you can't sing."

The man replied, "That's nothing. Fifty people have told me you can't preach, but you're still here.

All I am saying is that when we come to worship God in spirit and in truth, it won't take the choir to get you motivated. It won't take the preacher "whooping" to get your spirit stirred. But the hour cometh and now is here when the True Worshippers will worship God in spirit and in truth. And when we do this, souls will come alive.

God is seeking those who will worship in sincerity

1. God wants Sincerity in Purpose: David said in Psalm 5:7 "But as for me, I will come into thy house in the multitude of thy mercy: and in thy fear will I worship toward thy holy temple." David had the right motive and the correct purpose for his worship. It is crucial for all of us to be sincere in our purpose or motive for worshipping. People come to worship for different reasons. The Pharisees of Jesus's day just wanted to be seen and heard. They wanted to make a name for themselves, and they did just that. Jesus called them hypocrites. What a difference it would make if the believers all came together with singleness of purpose, and we turned our heart heavenward and worshipped the Lord.

2. God wants Sincerity in Practice: Does how we worship matter? Is it important? Absolutely. I have seen some practices involved in what was supposedly worship that made a mockery of God. What should be our guide in our worship practices? There is a mandate of the Scripture as to how we should worship. Our worship practices must include the magnification of the Savior. Does my worship glorify the Lord Jesus or does it draw attention to me? Our worship should be by the moving of the Spirit. Why am I worshipping in this manner? Is it because I have been moved by the Spirit or caught up in the flesh?

3. God wants Sincerity in Praise: Praise begins in the heart; the pure heart. God gets no satisfaction from those who shout in the church (but won't speak of Him or for Him in public). He is not blessed by lips that honor Him with a distant heart. Are we worshipping as God desires? Perhaps we need to evaluate our worship. Are we spirit filled? Are we sincere and genuine in our worship? When we worship we express our love for the Lord. True Worshippers will gain a sense of perspective of their own human limitations realizing that no matter what we're faced with, if I can just worship God, I

believe that the Holy Spirit will enter in… and take me to a spiritual place, where I can forget about myself. And concentrate on Him!

The criteria for effective Worship is that we must come to God with hearts cleansed from all unrighteousness. We must approach the Lord through the Blood and atonement found in Jesus. Our worship must be spiritual with pure spiritual motivations led by the Holy Spirit, which resides within us and according to the truth of the whole counsel of God found in the Bible.

- Worship must be done with increasing spiritual maturity and wisdom.
- Worship must be done first privately and then publicly.
- Worship must be done with all our heart, soul, strength, and mind.
- Worship must be done with great patience while waiting on the Lord to speak to us.
- Worship must be done with a teachable, humble, and available attitude.
- Worship must be done with a contrite and repentant heart.
- Worship must be done with love, trust, and a willingness to obey God in all things.
- Worship must be done with a sanctified lifestyle and willingness to know the Lord better.
- Worship must be done with a mind free of grudges or bitterness.

When Jesus entered into the temple on one Sabbath, the people were doing everything but worshipping. Jesus got so angry that He began tossing the furniture. God is willing to bless us abundantly as a church and individually. All He wants is for the True Worshippers to worship in Spirit and in Truth.

CHAPTER EIGHT

Where Are the True Worshippers?

John 4:20–24

This story begins in Chapter 4, verse 1, when Jesus had a need to go through Samaria. Understand that there are times when you need to go through some challenges that you would not wish on anyone. That Jesus is traveling through a place not many Jews would dare go through is very significant. For it was there that He met the woman at the well. This story can be viewed as not being so much about Him meeting the woman at the well, but more about what happened when they met. We find the heart of the story in verse 22. Jesus teaches a bit of doctrine; He finds a perfect opportunity to witness to someone unlike Him. He explains to the woman that "there is coming a time," and that time is now that the True Worshippers shall worship the Father in Spirit and in Truth.

Before I talk about Spirit and Truth, I want to first be clear on what Worship is. Worship usually means to bow down or to prostrate oneself out of respect. In simple terms, it means to reverence. Spirit is defined as a life-giving force or breath. An example is when God breathed in man's nostril. Truth is defined as fact, actuality, and correctness. To worship in Spirit and in Truth, it is important to know what Truth is. Scripture defines it as reality as God has revealed it. Truth in the Old Testament emphasizes reliability. Truth in the New Testament emphasizes reality. We can never experience the reality of Truth until we grasp God's reliable Word by faith and put them into practice. Jesus said in John 14:6, *"I am the way the truth and the life."* Therefore, it is critical for the true worshipper not to come for show, not to come for fashion, but when we come to the place of worship, we have got to be serious; we have got to worship God in Spirit and in Truth.

The question is, do we really know what true worship is all about? When we come together every week on Sunday morning, Sunday evening, and Wednesday evenings, we are coming together for a worship service. I am convinced that many of us do not know what a worship service really is. We come together and sing the songs of praise, but the song is not the worship. We love to hear the music, but the music itself is not the worship. All of these things are what we use to bring us into a place of worship, for true worship comes from the heart. Some folk believe that if they come to church on Sunday morning and force themselves to sing or to clap their hands every once in a while that they are worshipping God. But that is not what worshipping God is all about. The music, singing, clapping, or raising our hands and tapping our feet are all physical manifestations of worship. Before any of that can be considered worship, there has to be something even greater happening in the heart and in the Spirit.

Jesus gave us the meaning of true worship in verse 24, *"God is a Spirit: and they that worship him must worship him in spirit and in truth."* Real worship is totally surrendering your will to God's will in every area of your life. It is not giving part of your heart to God and then continuing to love the things of the world. It is not giving of your tithes and offerings yet holding back what God really wants you to give. Real worship isn't just coming to church; it is a lifestyle. The woman at the well had a form of worship. She was a religious woman who went to church all the time. It's similar to what Paul explained to Timothy in 2 Tim 3:5, *"Men will have only a form of godliness but deny the power thereof."* This church-going Samaritan realized that she needed something more. Maybe someone reading this feels like this woman—you have been attending church or some form of worship service, giving of your finances, getting your praise on, but you still feel a sense of emptiness.

So where are the true worshippers? The answers are not in the church building. The answers are not in the musical instruments. The answers are not in the preacher. The answers are found in the "living water" that only comes through a strong spiritual relationship and knowledge of Jesus Christ and a close walk with Him. We get into a competition when it comes to what we think real worship is. One church has better musicians than another. One church has a better choir than another. One church has a better praise team. One church has a better preacher. We forget that real worship doesn't come from watching somebody else worship. Real worship has to come from within your own heart and your own spirit. If you learn to worship God with your spirit and with your whole heart, none of that other stuff will be as important.

Jesus told the woman at the well: *"But the hour cometh, and now is, when the true worshippers shall worship the Father in spirit and in truth."* Why did he say this? Because the Father seeketh such to worship Him. True worship is displayed in living a life that is wholly dedicated to God. True worship can only come as we lose ourselves in Jesus. When you get lost in Jesus, and you begin to serve Him, praise Him, sing to Him, glorify Him, and forget about everything else, then you can begin to enter into real worship. One praise song says, "Forget about yourself and worship Him!" That's the kind of worship that we need, when we can forget about self, forget about yesterday, forget about tomorrow, and just worship Him in the moment.

You may ask what can I do to improve my worship? First, make worship God-centered. It really is not about you. Have you ever left a service saying, "I was really blessed by today's service"? Or have you ever left a service, all grumpy saying, "Boy, that was a waste of time. I didn't like the music, and I don't know what the pastor was talking about." This is because we have lost sight of something very important—worship is not primarily for us. While we may benefit from participating in public worship, it is not for us. Worship is for God and God alone. The question should not be, what do I get out of worship? But rather, what can I put into worship for God?

Secondly, you've got to prepare your heart beforehand. We bathe, get dressed, put on deodorant, comb our hair, and brush our teeth. All of this is preparation to come to worship, but what are you doing to prepare once you get in worship? Thirdly, you must arrive with a reachable heart. Determine that you are not going to arrive so frustrated and bent out of shape that it is virtually impossible for you to worship.

Then you've got to be determined to be a participant and not just a spectator. Worship is not something you watch. I know everybody does not worship in the same manner, but we all worship the same God. David said in Psalm 29:2, *"Worship God in the beauty of holiness."* The Lord said in Isaiah 66:23, *"All flesh shall come and worship before me."* Jesus even told satan in Matthew 4:10, *"You shall worship the Lord Your God."* Where are the True Worshippers? I am talking about the ones that don't mind getting ugly for the Lord, the ones that don't mind getting down on their knees, the ones that don't mind raising their hands, and don't mind stomping their feet. The ones willing to worship in Spirit and Truth—forgetting about self and worshipping Him!

CHAPTER NINE

Demons and Worship

Mark 5:18–20 NLT

I had just completed a series in Bible study dealing with strongholds. We discussed reasons for them; we discussed generational curses, and we discussed laying on of hands and casting out demons. And I said to the class, "If we can talk about and believe in angels and *angelology*, we also need to talk about and believe in demons and *demonology*."

As Jesus disembarks on the other side of the sea, the disciples fade from the story. A demon-possessed man takes center stage. He's possessed; he howls; he cuts himself with stones. His strength is such that no human figure can bind or control him. From his first encounter with Jesus, however, there is no question who is in control. Jesus is the strong one with the upper hand; the demonic trembles and asks that he be left alone. When it becomes apparent that Jesus will expel the demons (their name is Legion, for there are many of them), they ask instead to be sent into a nearby herd of swine. Jesus permits this, and the herd of pigs rushes headlong over the cliff into the lake and drowns. Verse 18 says the man begged Jesus to go with him, but Jesus did not allow it.

Jesus has just come through one of the most famous stories in the New Testament—the stilling of the storm on the sea. He has a desire now to go over to the Decapolis, an area just ten cities south of the Sea of Galilee (The Greek *deka* means ten). Each city has its own independent government; they were cities founded by Greek traders and immigrants, but over ninety-five percent of the people there were Gentiles. It is believed that Jesus wants to go over to the other side, as He said, to the Decapolis in order to do ministry in this large Gentile-populated area. When Jesus comes through the storm, and He gets to the other side, they encounter a man who is possessed by a demonic spirit. The text says the man runs to Jesus, bows before Him and worships Him.

As a pastor and a professor of theology, I had a problem with the text because we are told that this is a demon-possessed man, and yet the Bible says the demon-possessed man runs to Jesus and worships Him. This causes theological confusion because here is a man possessed by a demonic spirit, yet the text says he runs to Jesus and bows and worships the Lord. But when you put this into proper theology, you will discover how the demons in the manmade their mistake and lost their authority. We know that this action of worship can't be the demons because while demons believe, they don't worship—which means this has to be "the man in worship" with demons *in*. Did you hear what I just said? The man in worship had demons *in him*. If the demons who had been in control wanted to stay in control, the first mistake they made was not stopping the man from worshiping before they started talking. Truth be told, there have been moments when people have had demonic forces at work in their lives, and the first mistake the demons made was letting that person get to worship. Even with the devil in you, sometimes you make it through because you made it to worship. He is out of his mind but worshiping—not fully in his right mind— but worshiping. While he is out of his mind, obviously he has not lost his entire mind. So, the next time someone tells you "you have lost your mind," tell them, "Not all of it."

We discover in Mark's account of the story, the demon-possessed man had enough of his mind to get down on his knees and worship. If you really think about it, all you need is a piece of your mind. What ought to be your joy is the fact that after all you have been through, all you had to deal with at home or on the job that made you feel like you were losing your mind is that you still had enough sense to get to church and participate in worship. With everything you have on your mind, you have a justifiable reason to be crazy. There are people around you each and every day who just don't know that you are working a job, trying to keep your family together, trying to balance a budget, trying to be a parent, trying to pray, trying to worship, trying to keep focused, trying to be a leader, trying to be nice to people who are mean to you, and trying to speak to people who don't even deserve a handshake. You've got a lot going on, but you still have enough of your mind to know how to Worship!

Can I share a secret with you? If there is one thing that shakes the devil, it is not because you come to church. It is when you learn how to worship once you get in church. Because every time you worship, it reminds the devil that he has no power over you. Even that may not truly be the reason. why he can't stand your worship. I believe the real reason is because he messed up one time and got kicked out of heaven, and you mess up every day and took his place as a worshipper. The text reveals something to all of us that we should embrace. With all of the demonic presence in the demon-possessed man, he's got enough sense to worship. The Bible says Jesus takes authority over the demonic presence and the spirit of operation in man's mind, and the demons beg Jesus to send. them into the swine. What happens next is important because it is relevant to how our modern day society thinks: the owners of these pigs and the people were upset with Jesus and asked him to leave. They ask him to leave because they were more concerned over losing money than they were over celebrating the miracle of a man being healed. If the modern-day church doesn't stop being more concerned about money than it is about the souls of people, she will find herself wandering in the wilderness. They valued pigs over people, which in essence was valuing money over people. We cannot value things over people. The church is in danger when the money spent on our clothing is more than the money in the church budget. Obviously, the economic disruption in the text demonstrates that the people valued money more than this man's soul.

I am so glad that God still has a way to encourage us to follow Him, even after we have been possessed by all of our mess. In verse 18, the man makes a request of Jesus: "Let me go with you." When I read this, I said to myself: what better demonstration can Jesus have to teach a lesson? I could see how that could help His witness if the people saw this once demon-possessed man walk up to Jesus and let everybody see an ocular demonstration of

His supernatural power. I only imagined in my mind all of the possibilities for this fella— 'Let me be on one of the ministry teams; let me be one of the trustees; let me be the head Usher, better yet let me be a Deacon.' The Bible says Jesus denies his request. I am confused; the man has proven he is a worshiper. We know he has been cleaned up. We know his life has been turned around, and he's got a testimony. Why isn't he ready yet?

Because there are a whole lot of people in ministry, but they are not ready. There are a whole lot of members with titles, but they aren't ready. There are folks in the church with Superficial Holiness but no Practical Holiness, and they aren't ready. My question remains: Jesus, why isn't he ready? Jesus says before you will be ready to go with me, you must go home. Before you can go with me and be effective, you must go home and fix what you messed up. Because you have done a lot of damage when you were under demonic influence, I cannot let you think you can be effective until you fix what you messed up. This I believe is one of the reasons many preachers will not preach about family and about marriage because we want to be a public success, but we are fearful of being private failures. Many of us want positions and assignments in the church, but we are not ready. We want to follow Jesus, but we left our home in shambles. We want to lead Jesus's followers, but we refuse to lead our own families. I can imagine Jesus telling this once demon-possessed lunatic "You've got a story to tell, but you must first go home." The demonic was challenged to witness because he had a story to tell. We all have a story to tell. We are called by God to witness where we can do the best good.

In my book entitled *The Ministry of Missions,* I talk about how our story while witnessing can in fact encourage others; in fact, it can actually compel them to come to Jesus Christ knowing if He will help us through our challenges, just maybe He will help them through theirs. The greater your experience with the Lord, the more compelling the need to help others by letting God use you to do for them what was also done for you. There are individuals throughout scripture who had a story to tell. The woman who was thirsty but found the living waters had a story to tell and a duty to help others find that same fountain. The man who was destitute, jobless, and homeless had a story to tell and a duty to help others find the same saving

Lord that he had found. Jonah had a story to tell; he didn't want to tell it to the people of Nineveh, but he had to tell the story. Ezekiel had a story to tell. He had to tell the people that although they were dried up like dry bones in the valley, God could give them life again! Jeremiah had to tell it because it was like fire shut up in his bones. David had a story to tell. He had risen to lofty royal heights and had fallen to the depths of despair, yet he declared. *"The Lord is my shepherd I shall not want."* The lame man had a story to tell. He had been sitting by the pool for thirty-eight long years, but always missed his chance until one day Jesus told him to *"Take up that bed and walk!"* Your story might be: I was sinking deep in sin, but Jesus picked me up and turned me around. Your story might be I had a broken relationship, but He turned it around. Your story could be my finances were broken, but now I have more money than I could have even imagined. At some point in our lives, we have all had to face demons. It could be a sex demon, a gambling demon, a theft demon—whatever your demon was, if Jesus delivered you, first of all worship Him. Then, go back to the place where people know how you once were and witness to them by acknowledging that it was Jesus Christ who delivered you, and you now worship Him.

CHAPTER TEN

Authentic Worship

Philippians 3:3

"*For we are the circumcision, which worship God in the spirit, and rejoice in Christ Jesus, and have no confidence in the flesh.*" (KJV) Have you ever heard the phrase "We had church today"? It is a common phrase heard among African-American churchgoers. This indicates that all of the elements for God to be present were in place, and they were bathed with the spiritual power of God. In the African-American mindset, we *"have church"* when the worship is really touching, powerful, relevant, and meaningful. What makes such services valuable is the fact that through a combination of rhythmic, powerful preaching and a litany of songs and rituals that we praise God in such a way that we conclude, "We had church today." In our history as a people, "having church" meant following a prescribed ritual that no matter how meaningless or disconnected it was from the life we lived, it was still perceived as real worship. "Having church" required us to stand, sit, stand, sit, and then sing certain songs and talk back to the preacher; it even included a few shouts. When all of that happens at the same time, there are many who say, "Child, we show had church." Having church allows us to give the appearance of worship even while we participate in ungodly activities, which in themselves indicate that we are not in solidarity with the Savior, but simply participating in a ritual that feels good, offering no connectivity with the Savior. There is no harm with "having church," as long as it is not a substitute for real union with Christ. There is no harm in clapping our hands, as long as our hands are busy doing God's work. There is no harm with stomping our feet, as long as our feet are carrying us in the right direction. There is no harm in shouting every now and then, as long as we are shouting from within and not from without. I'm sure that among the old warriors that there were many who were on fire for God when they walked through the sanctuary doors. They were prayed up before they left home. They were in communion as they stood on the church grounds. They were "having church" long before the "call to worship." Real worship is in the heart and doesn't need a single ritual to make it happen. As Christians and believers, we worship God in Spirit and in Truth. It is not about organs, choir robes, pews, and singing *Amazing Grace*; it's about being connected with Christ in our spirit in a way that makes our worship authentic.

The story focuses on Paul as he explains that real worship does not depend on rituals, but on being in the spirit or in solidarity with Christ. The Jews had reduced worship to a series of meaningless rituals that substituted themselves for worship. These rituals included special hand washing ceremonies, special songs that were ordered, a variety of clothing that was specified or even special foods that were to be eaten or not eaten. Chief among the rituals was that of circumcision. Allow me to put a pin right there. Sometimes in the modern day Church, we get wrapped up in whether a person will go to heaven or not if they are not baptized. We get so hung up on the ritualistic or ceremonial part of baptism until we missed the most vital part to entering heaven—*salvation*. Men who were circumcised were considered in union with God. All adult males among Jews were required to show their allegiance and solidarity with God through circumcision. It was an outward ceremony that gradually became unique to the Jews. You do know baptism is an outward sign of an inward change. Circumcision was gender specific; it only applied to men because it was men who were intended to bring the sacrifices and participate in the ceremonies that indicated authentic worship. There was no similar requirement for women, indicating that worship was for men only. (That would not pass the litmus test in the modern Church.) Paul, however, addressed the ritual of circumcision by noting that true believers worship God not through rituals such as circumcision, but worship God in Spirit. If we depend on rituals and meaningless phrases, what we are doing now become legalism, and it is outward. It is not considered worship, however, because it only consists of outward acts, restricted to certain times and places.

Christian worship is spiritual, flowing from the in-workings of the Holy Spirit, not relating to certain isolated acts (feeding the homeless, visiting the sick, or comforting the downtrodden), but embracing the whole life. Circumcision represented a trust in human methods and traditions, but those who worship in spirit don't emphasize glorifying God in the flesh, but rather they promote glorifying Christ in the spirit. To truly worship, we must be in union with Christ. or connected with Him in all matters of truth. That truth will lead us to spiritual freedom, a truth that Jesus says, *"will make you free."* Our worship must have an impact on those around us; authentic worship makes an impact on believers and non-believers. The world takes notice when the Church, in solidarity with Christ, worships Him by precept, example, song, and prayer. Authentic worship causes a couple of things to happen.

Authentic worship attracts, and authentic worship is spontaneous.

1. *Authentic worship attracts.* If our worship is meaningful and not just an empty ritual, it will get the attention of non-believers. When believers are excited about worship, the sincerity of their songs and praise attracts non-believers, who want to know how to change their lives to feel the same excitement. This is why choirs can't sing the praises unto God with sour faces. People are watching. Musicians can't play their instruments with a nonchalant attitude. People are watching. Ushers can't greet people with "I don't want be here" attitudes. People are watching. True believers praise God and thank Him for everything, even our adversities. The Psalmist declares that no matter what life throws at you, everything that has breath should praise God. Why do you think we call it *Praise* and *Worship?* Because we praise God for what He has done, and we worship Him for who He is. If you can't praise Him, it is next to impossible to worship Him. Why? Because if He has never done anything for you, you have no reason to praise Him. And if you have no reason to praise

Him, you have no reason to believe He is who He says He is. But I'm sure if you would just pause for a moment and think back over your life, you more than likely would testify that He is:

- Jehovah Jireh because He has provided for you.
- He is Jehovah Rapha because He healed your body.
- He is Jehovah Shalom because when everything around you was crazy, He gave you peace that passes all understanding.

When the unsaved see the Church thanking God for the unseen spiritual blessings of salvation, they are drawn to the faith by an invisible attraction that tugs at their soul. This is *Authentic Worship*. It's a powerful picture. We praise Him for the seen and the unseen. In solidarity with Christ, we should praise Him for the greens and the butter beans, our little car, and our house. I remember when I used to drive my old, beat-up truck to church; some folk made light of my jalopy. But I kept on praising God anyhow, thanking Him that at least I had transportation. Authentic worship will attract others.

2. *Authentic worship is spontaneous.* Those who have learned how to live their lives connected with God, worship Him spontaneously. There is no set time for them to lift Him up. There is no set place to lift Him up; you can praise while sitting in your car parked at the red light. When the saints of God get together, those who really know the Lord don't even need a Call to Worship because authentic worship is from the heart. It is spontaneous; it cannot be orchestrated. We clap when we are moved to clap, not because we are told. We stand on our feet, wave our hands, or even get our dance on when we are moved to do so. It's whenever our hearts demand that we respond. It has no particular order; it comes as the Spirit gives utterance. Some may cry; some may shout; some may sit still and soak in the atmosphere. Others may dance the holy dance. No

> matter what method is used, authentic worship is from the heart. It comes spontaneously when believers are in solidarity with Christ. Sometimes when you lift Him up with joy continuously, day after day, because you love Him, people who really don't love the Lord will criticize you for constantly praising God. We must remember that true praise cannot be contained. When true believers think about God's grace and mercy, we have to worship Him all over again. We try our best to be civilized and to hold back our feelings, but when we think about all the things God has done for us, it's hard to hold your peace. We must worship Him in Spirit and Truth. It's hard to hold your peace when we think about the grace of God.

There is a story I once heard about an old grandmother who moved in with her great- grandchildren up north. They were wealthy professionals who attended a quiet church in a big city. Her grandchildren went to church regularly, but they asked Grandmother to remember that she wasn't down south. "Folks up here don't say 'Amen' and stuff like they do down south. Don't embarrass us." Every Sunday the old lady went to worship and tried her best to keep quiet as the name of Jesus was glorified. Her grandchildren would give her the eye, and she would hold her peace. They didn't mind the funny looking red coat she wore. They didn't mind the flower that dangled from her hat. If she'd just sit quietly, they'd be happy. One day a guest preacher from down south was in the pulpit. He began talking about the goodness of the Lord. As he talked, the flower started dangling on the old lady's hat as she moved from side to side. Her heels started tapping on the floor. Before she knew it, she was standing on her feet shouting. As her embarrassed grandchildren stared at her, along with the whole church, she put her hands on her mouth and said, "I'm sorry, y'all, but I just got to praise the Lord!"

I must admit, there are times when I just can't keep it to myself; I've got to tell somebody about the goodness of the Lord. Tell somebody about a Savior who picked me up and turned me around. Tell somebody about a risen Savior who tells me I am His own. His name is Jesus the Christ.

CHAPTER ELEVEN

The Worship War

Luke 4:13

The definition of a temptation is an urge or desire to do something, especially something you should not, or it refers to a wrong or forbidden pleasure that is enticing. It's been said, "I wouldn't be tempted if temptation wasn't so tempting." Oscar Wilde described it this way, "I can resist anything, except temptation." There's a story about a boy in a grocery store, which illustrates the nature of temptation quite nicely. It seems the boy was standing near an open box of peanut butter cookies when the grocer approached him.

"Now then, young man," said the grocer, "what are you up to?"

"Nothing," replied the boy.

"Well, it looks to me like you were trying to take a cookie," the grocer said as he pointed to the open box.

"Oh, you're so wrong, mister. I'm trying not to!"

Now that's temptation—I'm trying not to. Maybe you've heard someone say, "The devil made me do it." Granted, it began as a joke, but some may think it's a convenient defense to blame it on the devil. But there's just one problem: the devil cannot make us do anything. He can tempt us but not force us. On the other hand, it may feel different when your faith and your desires disagree.

Lucifer's primary goal and strategy are to make them disagree. Primarily, he wants us to disagree about Jesus. A minister once pointed out that, "All the warnings in the New Testament concerning conflicts with Satan are addressed only to believers. Why? Because Satan doesn't want us to believe

God." Satan is committed to doing whatever's necessary to make us ineffective, in our personal lives and in our personal ministries. By doubting the Father or the Son, we doubt both. That makes us ineffective. James 1:13 says, *"When tempted, no one should say, 'God is tempting me.' For God cannot be tempted by evil, nor does he tempt anyone;[14] but each one is tempted when, by his own evil desire, he is dragged away and enticed."* What are you talking about, Rowden—"dragged away" from what? He's dragged away from faith in God. When we give into temptations, we reveal a lack of faith that God can protect us from temptation.

Notice that I said, "protect us from temptation" and not "keep us from being tempted." In this world, temptations are everywhere. Some are huge; some are small, but none of them are from God, *"for God does not tempt anyone."* The strategy behind temptation is to make us ineffective witnesses for Christ. If we are ineffective, we hurt others and especially the Church. The enemy knows full well that he was defeated at the Cross, but he's fully committed to dragging as many of us down with him as he can. He doesn't fight fair. He fights a spiritual war, and that's the real battlefield, the spiritual realm. And if you don't have the Spirit of God inside of you, the enemy will win every time. 1 Peter 5:8–9 exhorts us to *"Be self-controlled and alert. Your enemy the devil prowls around like a roaring lion seeking someone to devour. Resist him, standing firm in the faith."*

Unfortunately, far too many people have the wrong idea concerning the word "resist." Somewhere along the way, "resisting Satan" was changed to "ignore Satan," or better yet for Satan, just don't believe that he exists at all. You know the expression, "Keep your friends close and your enemies closer." The logic of those words lies in the reality that you should never underestimate the damage the enemy can do when you don't know what he's doing. By denying the existence of real evil, you empower it. When you define temptation as nothing more than a "natural urge" or an "innocent mistake," you fail to see the true damage it can do emotionally and spiritually. Where did we ever get the idea that the best approach to dealing with Satan is to dismiss and ignore him as nothing more than a fantasy or a theological myth? Standing against the enemy's attacks is not a task to be taken lightly. Our enemy is a cunning and relentless adversary. His mastery of evil enables him to fashion lewd temptations or fling fiery darts with amazing accuracy.

He may not have the power to read your mind, but then, he doesn't have to. He already knows your basic nature, and all he has to do is appeal to it. Job, Joshua, Daniel, David, and the apostle Paul were men who had real and convincing experiences that proved that they were not immune to the wiles of a very real Tempter. If these great saints of the Bible were vulnerable, what makes you think you are the exception? The greatest example of Satan's audacity was his attempt to deceive the Son of God in the wilderness. If he's bold enough to get in the face of Christ, why should we expect him to steer clear of us? The writer of Hebrews lays before us this truth: *"For we do not have a high priest who cannot sympathize with our weakness, but was in all points tempted as we are, yet without sin." (*Hebrews 4:15) our real battle is to be true to the purpose for which you were created. To win the "Worship War" against temptation takes the power of God, which was given to you in the Holy Spirit, a power the enemy doesn't want you to recognize, let alone use the gifts the Holy Spirit gives you to win. He wants you to stay in bondage and in defeat. Christians are called to be the spiritually commissioned and empowered army of God, demonstrating the power of God by living victorious, fruitful, and godly lives.

There are powers of darkness in this world that are seeking to neutralize the followers of Christ at all cost. This is the whole reason for the many attacks against Christians, especially against those Believers who are responding to God's call, those who are brave enough to take a stand of faith in God's Word. There are things we can do to be prepared for battle in the spiritual realm. Some things I believe will help in "The Worship War Against Temptation." First, we must cultivate humility and obedience. Scripture presents humility as a divine *requirement and an endearing characteristic for all Christians. The prophet Micah, in 6:8, shares this truth, "The Lord has already told you what is good, and this is what he requires: to do what is right, to love mercy, and to walk humbly with your God."* Pride was the reason for Satan's fall. This is why Peter warns us that God abhors pride and desires humility. If you want to resist temptation, you need to make sure that you're not *"putting up a barrier"* with God due to pride. The most common barrier today—even among Christians—is our attitude. Humility comes from acknowledging that the real battle is spiritual, and we need spiritual power in order to win. Humility and wisdom come from admitting that the spiritual war is real, and we cannot win without the power of the Holy Spirit.

Humility must also be combined with obedience. The prophet Samuel declared that, "*To obey is better than sacrifice.*" Why? For one simple reason: with sacrifice, we decide what God will get, but with obedience, God decides, and we obey. *"To obey is better than sacrifice."*

The second protection for the spiritual battle is our spiritual armor, accompanied by spiritual accountability. It's astonishing how many confessing Christians live their lives without wearing their spiritual armor, and then they wonder why things keep going wrong. The most common reason seems to be simple carelessness. People just don't think about putting on their spiritual armor. Yet Paul is clear: spiritual armor is not an optional accessory. Those who choose to dismiss it do so at their own peril. Paul summed it up in four simple words: *"I die every day."* (1 Corinthians 15:31 ESV) Let me say that again: "I die every day." Rather than visualizing literal helmets, breastplates, and shields, simply dedicate your first conscious thoughts each morning to the will of God. Spiritual armor becomes a lifestyle when we choose to consciously walk in the presence of God daily, but spiritual armor also requires spiritual accountability. Spiritual accountability with each other helps each of us to establish guardrails—safety lines in case we stumble. The Scriptures state this clearly in Hebrews 10:25. Our recent Bible study text, *"And let us not neglect our meeting together, as some people do, but encourage and warn each other...."* We have got to be humble and accountable to one another.

Thirdly: a faithful prayer life must be a part of the battle plan. Nearly all of our failures are prayer failures. James encourages us to pray without ceasing; *"Men ought to always pray."* Think about it, when was the last time you really sought God in prayer, other than at this altar or when you were asking God for a favor?

The final protection is to take godly risks. Many Christians overlook this because they think of "risk" as something to avoid. I can remember years ago when I first started investing in stocks; they asked me what level of risk did I want to take? I had no idea what they were talking about. The broker explained: low, medium, or high risk determines the return on my investment. The higher the risk, the greater chance for higher return on the investment, and the lower the risk, naturally, the lower the investment. But when it comes to taking "godly risks," the real danger is often in the realm of just maintaining the status quo—not rocking the boat, being politically correct. If we are to succeed on the spiritual battlefield, we must learn to walk in faith. And for the Christian, faith is not spelled "f-a-i-t-h"; it's spelled "r-i-s-k." If there's no risk involved, then it really doesn't require faith. Hebrews 11:6 tells us, *"without faith it is impossible to please God."* So a risk-free life is a life without victory. A risk-free life means a lifelong surrender to mediocrity—which, in a way, is the worst of all possible deaths. Satan and his army are a real-and-present danger. Temptations will come—and keep on coming. But you've got to learn how to fight this "Worship War Against Temptations."

Praise is the Expression We Give

To the Worship We Live.

Created for Worship is a guide for those desiring a closer walk with the Master through worship. There are individuals that attend "worship services" weekly yet are unfamiliar with True Worship. People worship in many different ways: however, the method, it must be "in spirit and in truth." *Created for Worship* will stimulate meaningful discussion about why we worship, how we worship, when should we worship, and an overall **worship** practice. Worship comes in many forms: public worship, private worship, and cooperate worship just to name a few. "But the time is coming—indeed it's here now—when true worshipers will worship the Father in spirit and in truth. The Father is looking for those who will worship him that way. For God is Spirit, so those who worship him must worship in spirit and in truth." (John 4:23, 24 NLT)

Mark Rowden is a visionary Pastor, Professor of Theology, evangelist, community leader, educator, retired veteran, and patriarch to his family. *Created for Worship* was birthed from a deep commitment for worshipping the one true God. Dr. Rowden felt a strong sense of sharing his personal worship experiences with those who want a better understanding of "God *is* Spirit, and those who worship Him must worship in spirit and truth." (John 4:24) Dr. Rowden and his wife, Beverly, are worshippers and enjoy being in the presence of God in worship. Dr. Rowden serves as senior pastor of the Savannah Missionary Baptist Church located in Fayetteville, North Carolina and is the Founder/President of the Mark Rowden Ministry International, Inc., a global ministry of outreach also headquartered in Fayetteville. Dr. Rowden has a passion for helping others grow in their relationship with the Savior and is committed to the teachings of the gospel of Jesus Christ. Dr. Rowden truly believes when God's people worship in spirit and in truth and do it with full trust in Him, it is then they experience the fullness of the Lord's blessings, healings, and deliverance.

About the Author

Mark A. Rowden is a pastor, professor of theology, and Army veteran. He is the author of The Ministry of Missions — Missions is Ministry. He is a native of Houston, Texas. He is the recipient of the 2014 Religious Leader of the Year Award and in 2021 The Order of the Long Leaf Pine by the Governor of North Carolina. Dr. Rowden is the Site President for the North Carolina Theological Seminary at Cumberland County in Fayetteville, North Carolina. Dr. Rowden is an international preacher and teacher who has carried the Gospel to Bahrain (Middle East), Bosnia (Europe), Korea (Asia), West and South Africa, and India, the U.S. Virgin Islands, and Hawaii. Dr. Rowden serves as a regional representative for the National Baptist Convention, USA, Inc. Foreign Missions Board for North Carolina, South Carolina, Florida, Georgia, and Virginia. Pastor Rowden is the Admin Chaplain for the Cumberland County Sheriff's office where he provides spiritual support to over 350 sworn deputies, detention officers, civilians, and inmates. Pastor Rowden is servant leader of Savannah Missionary Baptist Church of Fayetteville, NC and is the Founder/President of Mark Rowden Ministry, International, Inc. He is married to Beverly Knox Rowden, also of Houston, Texas.

www.ingramcontent.com/pod-product-compliance
Ingram Content Group UK Ltd.
Pitfield, Milton Keynes, MK11 3LW, UK
UKHW020122230720
13967UKWH00007B/2768

9 781649 907578